steuben design

steuben design

a legacy
of light and form

M.J. MADIGAN

Harry N. Abrams, Inc., Publishers

FOR ANN LESLIE KEOHAN MADIGAN

EDITOR: Andrea Danese
PRODUCTION MANAGER: Maria Pia Gramaglia
BOOK & COVER DESIGN: Abbott Miller with Johnschen Kudos, Pentagram

This book was set in Neutraface by House Industries

Library of Congress Cataloging-in-Publication Data
Madigan, Mary Jean Smith.
Steuben design : a legacy of light and form
by M. J. Madigan, Marie McKee.
        p. cm.
Includes bibliographical references and index.
ISBN 0-8109-4645-9
1. Steuben Glass, inc.—Catalogs. 2. Crystal glass—United
States—History—20th century—Catalogs. 3. Cut glass—United
States—Catalogs. I. McKee, Marie. II. Title.

NK5205.S75A4 2004
748.2'09747'83—DC22
2003020740

Copyright © 2004 by Corning Incorporated

Published in 2004 by Harry N. Abrams, Incorporated, New York.
All rights reserved. No part of the contents of this book may be
reproduced without written permission of the publisher.

Printed and bound in China

Harry N. Abrams, Inc.
100 Fifth Avenue
New York, N.Y. 10011
www.abramsbooks.com

Abrams is a subsidiary of

LA MARTINIÈRE
GROUPE

FRONTISPIECE Set on a windowsill in the Steuben design department offices
at 717 Fifth Avenue, Angus McDougall's Apple refracts a perfect inverted
image of the Manhattan cityscape at Fifth Avenue and 56th Street, ca. 1977.

TITLE PAGE First patented as the company's trademark in 1950, the Steuben
Snowflake was designed by Philip Grushkin to symbolize nature's perfect
crystal—and Steuben's.

contents

foreword

When I became president of Steuben Glass in 1998, I took certain things for granted. After all, Steuben's reputation as purveyor of "the world's purest crystal" had been established for many decades. Steuben designs have been honored White House Gifts of State since the 1940s, and gifts of choice for engagements and marriages, graduations and promotions, retirements, anniversaries, births, and milestones of every description both public and private since our company was founded one hundred years ago. Prestigious museums collect Steuben crystal, connoisseurs covet and cherish it, and critics praise it for purity of form and joy of use.

I knew all of these things when I arrived at Steuben. Then my real education began.

What I have learned—and what this book celebrates—is that the enduring value of Steuben crystal resides in something intangible but palpably present in every piece: An amalgam of talent, experience, inspiration, and love is transferred from the hearts and hands of the people who make the object to the recipient of their gifts. Steuben is alone in America in its continuing dedication to a single ancient material and its passionate commitment to ages-old techniques for making the most extraordinary glass. We believe that no matter how skilled a society becomes at mass production and planned obsolescence, the most cherished objects will always be those made one at a time by the human hand.

Moreover, I have come to see that superior design can have a profound effect upon everyday life. This is a core value for our company, the wellspring of meaning for an authentic and successful business, and it is as relevant today as ever. Through advanced technique, design excellence, and the inherent majesty of glass as a material, we at Steuben express our confidence in the enduring, transformative power of great design.

In past centuries, handmade glass objects were prized as the keys to a dowry or the jewels of an inheritance. Such treasures moved in time from workshops to homes and palaces, to museums, and ultimately into the canon of history. Because glass is unique in its potency as a vessel for emotion and insight, and because the best design can challenge and delight, the objects we fashion from glass today are equally essential. They convey our story as a society into the future, rendering their authors stewards of our memories, aspirations, and traditions. At Steuben, we view this as a wonderful privilege.

Steuben artists and designers are a family. Through their generous pragmatism and spirited explorations we forge connections to an ever-expanding community beyond our own. We build relationships upon collections of simply beautiful objects that increase pleasure and mark the passage of time. Today's creative solution becomes tomorrow's heirloom: Imbued with life-affirming effervescence, Steuben crystal passes from our hands to those of future generations.

In our next century, Steuben's designers and artists will continue to make objects that elicit a sense of the sublime. From our family to yours, welcome!

Marie McKee, President and CEO, Steuben Glass

portfolio 1

Glimmer Old-Fashioned Glass, Glimmer Highball Glass, Taffeta Vase, Teardrop Bud Vase, Small Folded Bo
Bouquet Vase, Small Orbit Bowl, Classic Highball Glass, Classic Old-Fashioned Glass.

living with steuben

Made in America for one hundred years, Steuben glass brings the uplifting presence of the glassmaker's art into the lives and homes of discerning people everywhere. Each piece of consummately pure Steuben crystal is a perfect marriage of art and function. It can be a versatile vessel, a meditative focus for one's thoughts, a window on an exotic world, or a dazzling piece of sculpture, alive with light. Whatever form it takes, Steuben glass has the power to illuminate and transform its surroundings, magnifying the simple joys of everyday living.

In the exuberant decades of the mid-twentieth century, Steuben's name became synonymous with glamour and style. Its exquisite glass for the table and home became an indispensable accouterment to the elegant entertaining that defined sophisticated lifestyles during those heady years. "To have Steuben glass in your home or on your table will register you among those who know the right things," observed the redoubtable Walter Dorwin Teague, who personally designed a collection of tableware for Steuben in the early 1930s.

In this spirit, Steuben has introduced a new line of stemware, barware, and drinking accessories inspired by the glamour and style of the 1930s, 1940s, and 1950s—the first major collection of such pieces to be offered in more than a generation. As a salute to midcentury design, a collection of classic functional pieces by George Thompson—a leading member of Steuben's design atelier from 1936 to 1974—has been returned to production.

Today, as in years past, Steuben's place at the forefront of glassmaking artistry remains unchallenged—a tribute to the purity of its crystal, the skill of its craftspeople, and the classic elegance of its timeless designs.

The glamorous Mrs. John Monteith Gates, wife of Steuben's managing director, poses with Steuben table crystal. This ad shot by fashion photographer John Rawlings was featured in the July 1942 issue of *Vogue*.

George Thompson designed the Rope-twist Candlesticks in 1939 to emphasize the graceful flowing character of pure crystal.

OPPOSITE In 1953, Donald Pollard created this simple and elegant Heritage Liqueur Decanter with its asymmetrical rim and air-trap stopper, accompanied by a set of four pristine Liqueur Glasses.

Designed by George Thompson in 1940, the Heritage Lotus Vase has a base formed from eight separate bits of glass to suggest an unfolding lotus blossom.

OPPOSITE David Dowler's set of Skyline Candlesticks from 2000—like the functional designs of the 1940s and 1950s—exploits the unique brilliance and transparency of pure Steuben crystal.

OPPOSITE George Thompson's classic Bouquet Vase, designed with a cinched waist to hold flower stems in an upright position, is a classic example of the simple, supremely functional pieces that dominated Steuben design at midcentury. First introduced in 1949, the Bouquet Vase has remained in constant production.

ABOVE LEFT Smaller versions of the Olive Dish designed by John Dreves for the 1939 World's Fair, George Thompson's little Nut Bowls were first introduced in 1947 and brought back into the line as a pair to mark Steuben's 100th anniversary in 2003.

ABOVE RIGHT The Air-twist Decanter, another George Thompson design, was first introduced in 1949 and reintroduced during Steuben's centenary. Its distinctive stopper is hand-formed with a technique often employed by Steuben's skilled glassblowers in the 1940s.

portfolio 2

Forever More, Owl, Equestrian Decanter, Evening Champagne Glass, Lion, Regal

Steuben's founder, English glassmaster Frederick Carder, ran the firm
and designed virtually all its glass for 30 years. Seated in his office
ca. 1930, the dapper Carder sketches an engraving design for a goblet,
surrounded by examples of his exuberant art glass.

an american legacy

Steuben Glass takes pride in its deeply American roots. Founded in 1903 in Corning, New York, by expatriate English glassmaker Frederick Carder and local businessman Thomas Hawkes, it is named for the county where Corning is located. From the start, Carder ran all aspects of the operation, producing a wide range of iridescent, colored, and engraved art glass that is now avidly collected as Carder Steuben.

During World War I, Steuben was sold to Corning Glass Works, now Corning Incorporated. Carder continued at the helm until 1933, when he was succeeded by Arthur Amory Houghton Jr.—the young Harvard-educated great-grandson of Corning Glass Works' founder. Urbane, patrician, and sensitive to changing tastes, Houghton gradually discontinued Carder's colored glass, seizing on a newly discovered glass formula of exceptional clarity and brilliance to make the pure, color-free crystal for which Steuben is best known today. With a credo of uncompromising excellence in materials, design, and craftsmanship, he vowed to create "the most perfect crystal the world has ever known."

Catering to people of style and means, Houghton opened the first of three successive shops on New York's fashionable Fifth Avenue in 1934, followed by Steuben Glass galleries in fine stores across America. Renowned artists such as Georgia O'Keeffe, Giorgio de Chirico, Isamu Noguchi, and others contributed drawings for copper-wheel engraving on the crystal—a centuries-old craft that is preserved to this day by Steuben artisans. In 1947, President Truman presented England's Princess Elizabeth with a wedding gift of Steuben; since then, every U.S. president has chosen Steuben crystal as America's gift of state. Outstanding examples of Steuben's artistry are found in the collections of major museums in America and around the globe.

In its upstate New York factory, Steuben glass is still handmade one piece at a time by skilled glassworkers, some from families who have been making glass in Corning for generations. Each perfect piece is destined to become a uniquely American heirloom, gracing the homes and tables of generations to come.

Henning Overstrom was the first glassblower hired in 1903. Carder lured Swedish-born craftsmen away from Dorflinger and other American glass manufactories when union problems prevented him from bringing over English glassworkers.

Steuben's first factory was in a converted foundry on Erie Avenue, next to the rail lines that connected Corning to Pennsylvania coal fields and markets in New York City and the West. Within a decade of this 1908 photo, Steuben employed 27 glassworkers and occupied several buildings.

FROM LEFT Steuben's second furnace, constructed in 1908, could melt 16 pots of glass set into its arched bays. This enabled the company to expand its output to make lighting fixtures, tableware, colored art glass, and cut crystal. A young "carry-in boy" assists the "gaffer," or master glassblower, at his bench.

In 1932, due to deterioration at the Erie Avenue plant, Steuben moved to "B" factory of the main Corning Glass Works. Here, a glassmaking "shop," or team, works near its reheating furnace, or "glory hole."

The finishing room at the Erie Avenue plant around 1910 shows the wide range of decorative glass and tablewares being turned out by Carder just seven years after the company was founded. Polishing and grinding wheels were powered by a single overhead drive shaft.

OPPOSITE Steuben was revolutionized in the years after 1933 by a young and suave triumvirate: architect John Monteith Gates, Arthur Amory Houghton Jr., and designer Sidney Waugh. Around a table elegantly appointed with Steuben barware and stemware, they discuss Waugh's sketch for his 1938 Hercules Vase.

ABOVE The interior of Steuben's first shop at 478 Fifth Avenue, a former Sherry's restaurant, as it appeared shortly after opening in 1934. Some remaining stock of colored Carder glass is on display along with pieces of the new colorless crystal designed by Arthur Dorwin Teague and Sidney Waugh, whose illuminated Gazelle Fountain sculpture is seen in the niche at rear.

OPPOSITE In 1937, the Steuben shop moved south to 718 Fifth Avenue, where it occupied the street and mezzanine levels of the new Corning Glass building, a modernist edifice designed by Platt and Platt Architects and faced with blocks of Corning's Pyrex glass. Sidney Waugh designed the sculptural detailing on the building's facade.

ABOVE By the late 1930s, Steuben had recruited a group of talented young designers, many of them trained in architecture, for its first design department. Here they are shown at work in their atelier in the Corning Glass building at 718 Fifth Avenue.

Sidney Waugh poses with Atlantica, the 300-pound cast-crystal sculpture he designed for Steuben's exhibit at the 1939 World's Fair. Nearly three million people filed through the fair's Steuben display between April and October of that year.

ABOVE A stylishly turned-out customer chats with Arthur Houghton at a 1948 cocktail reception, one of many held to mark glass introductions and to launch special exhibitions in the New York shop.

RIGHT Steuben's managing director John Gates chats with participating artist Georgia O'Keeffe at the 1940 opening of Steuben's landmark "Twenty-seven Artists in Crystal" exhibition at the New York shop. In addition to O'Keeffe, twenty-six renowned artists including Henri Matisse, Grant Wood, André Derain, Salvador Dalí, and Isamu Noguchi were commissioned to create drawings to be copper-wheel engraved on Steuben plates, vases, and bowls.

In 1951, Steuben moved its glass-making operations to a new factory attached to the innovative new Corning Glass Center. For the first time, visitors could tour the factory and watch crystal being made. The large black Robinson ventilators at the top of the building help to dissipate rising heat from the glory holes and melting tank.

In the 1940s and 1950s, Steuben organized a series of international glass exhibitions to educate the public and increase its visibility. It also participated in "L'Art du Verre," a show sponsored by the Louvre in 1951 to celebrate glassmaking's postwar regeneration. John Gates designed Steuben's display, seen here, which comprised a fifth of the entire exhibition in the Palais du Louvre.

Inside the new Steuben factory, ca. 1951, each shop of glassworkers worked around its own glory hole under the direction of the gaffer.

OPPOSITE The Steuben shop moved across the street to the new Corning Building at 717 Fifth Avenue in March 1959, from its familiar glass-block building (far right foreground). At the time, it was the highest glass-walled skyscraper in New York City.

OPPOSITE The interior of Steuben's new shop, ca. 1959, featured a fountain by staff designer George Thompson, who also designed this crystal Cascade Wall, a room divider toward the rear suspended over a reflecting pool.

ABOVE Visiting schoolchildren delight in a veritable Noah's Ark of Steuben animals, on display at a special "Animal Fair" exhibition at the 717 Fifth Avenue shop in 1971.

During the 1980s, Steuben invited well-known architects and designers to spend time in the Corning factory and create special designs as part of an ongoing visiting artists program. Here, architect Michael Graves helps shear the rim from a piece in his 1989 Archaic Vessels collection.

In 2000 the Steuben flagship store moved from Fifth Avenue to a new three-level shop designed by Ralph Applebaum at 667 Madison Avenue. Architect Paul Haigh conceived the ground-level interior showroom seen in this photograph taken in 2003.

portfolio 3

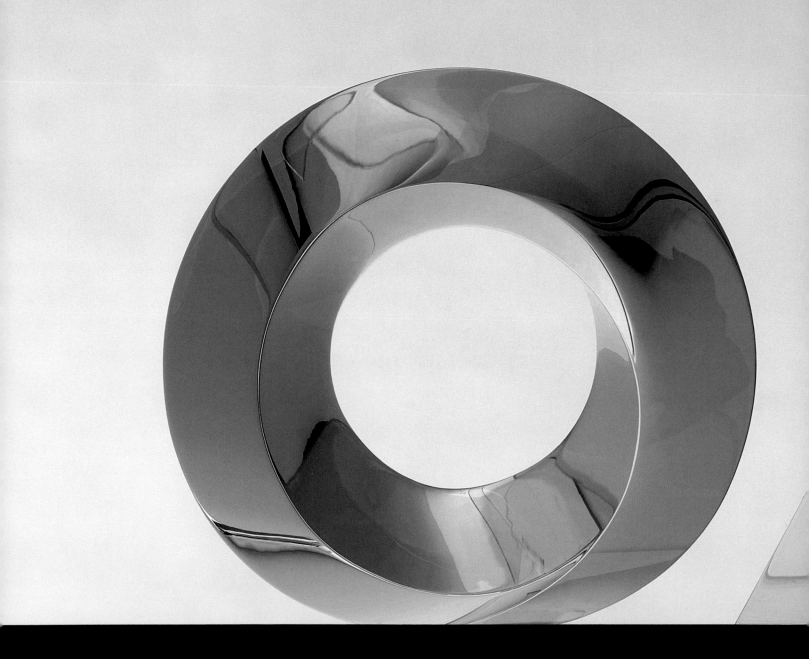

Heart Point Down, Heart Point Up, Mobius Prism, Sailboat, Stars

an ageless alchemy

First practiced more than 3,500 years ago in Mesopotamia and ancient Egypt, glassmaking is an astounding process. When melted together at high heat, the common materials of sand and potash, combined with a stabilizer such as lime, are magically transformed into a unique substance that flows like a viscous liquid in its molten state, then cools into a transparent solid that both reflects and refracts light. In the 17th century, the Englishman George Ravenscroft made the first crystal (or "flint" glass) by adding pure lead to the traditional recipe. This created a heavy glass of great transparency and brilliance that could be worked longer before solidifying, enabling craftsmen to make objects of greater complexity.

Today, visitors to the Steuben Glass factory at Corning, New York, can observe crystal being made by hand with methods and tools little changed from those in use centuries ago. Technological advances like gas-fired furnaces and computer-fed melting tanks have refined the ancient process, achieving a glass of extraordinary purity and brilliance that is unmatched by any crystal in the world.

In keeping with age-old tradition, glassmaking at Steuben is a team effort. Each team or "shop" works near its designated reheating furnace or "glory hole," directed by a master glassblower called a "gaffer" (a term thought to be a corruption of the word grandfather). Each shop specializes in a number of specific designs assigned to no other team. This system ensures the consistency and perfection of each piece of Steuben, though it may increase the customer's wait for an especially popular design.

At Steuben, uncompromising perfection is the standard. Each completed piece of crystal is rigorously inspected. If any flaw is discovered, the piece will be shattered. Steuben sells no seconds.

Molten crystal uniformly heated to 2500 degrees Fahrenheit flows constantly from the base of Steuben's large melting tank into a stream of chilled water in the "cave," or cellar, below. When a "gather" of glass is needed, a metal cup catches a portion of the flow, timed in seconds to ensure consistent sizing of specific pieces (for example, the Olive Dish requires a 53-second pour). Between gathers, the molten stream flows into the running water, cools, and is broken into cullet, which is fed back into the melting tank.

From the cellar beneath the melting tank, a measured gather of hot glass is hoisted up to the blowing-room floor.

OPPOSITE A servitor removes the hot gather from its metal cup and carries it at the end of a metal blowing iron to his shop's reheating furnace or glory hole, where it will be hand-formed by the gaffer. At this stage the glass has cooled to a 1,500-degree working temperature.

OPPOSITE TOP A cherrywood paddle is used to shape the sides of the parison as it is rotated across a metal bar to prevent sagging. It will be transferred from the blowpipe to a long solid "punty" (or pontil rod) for further hand-forming by the gaffer.

OPPOSITE BELOW As it is being worked, the parison of glass is thrust repeatedly into the gas-fired glory hole to maintain a constant temperature. The door to the glory hole is equipped with apertures of various sizes. The smaller square opening allows glassworkers to keep the tips of the glassworking rods hot.

LEFT The servitor rolls the glowing, viscous mass back and forth on a "marver" (or metal surface) to make it uniform and cool the surface before blowing.

ABOVE With a quick puff of air, the servitor creates a bubble of glass or "parison" at the end of the blowpipe. This is the basic element from which all hand-blown or "at the fire" pieces are formed.

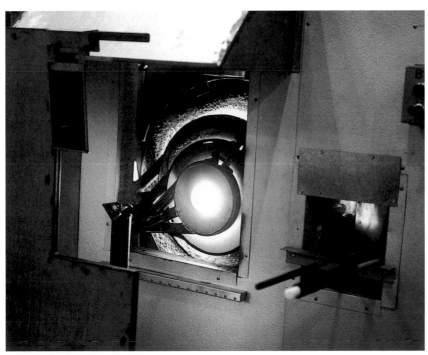

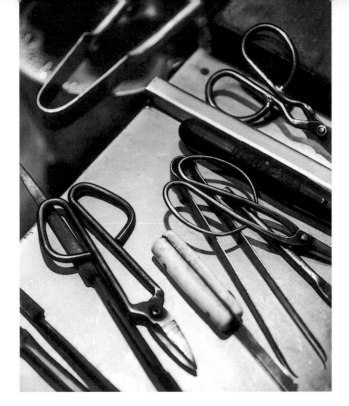

ABOVE The basic glassmaker's tools—including the shears and calipers of various sizes shown here—have changed remarkably little through the centuries.

OPPOSITE AND RIGHT Using metal shears, the gaffer cuts away unwanted glass from the rim of a bowl. When the bowl is fully shaped, the gaffer uses "bit shears" to guide the application of a bit of hot glass from the servitor's rod to form the bowl's decorative handle.

ABOVE When the glass is fully formed but still about 400 degrees hot, it is "cracked off" the punty with a single sharp blow and carried with asbestos gloves to the "lehr," or annealing oven. There, like the Butterflies shown, it is carried on a moving belt through a controlled atmosphere of slowly decreasing temperatures. This slow annealing prevents the glass from cracking as it cools.

RIGHT Cooled-down objects emerge in the adjacent finishing area. Here, a glassworker grinds down rough surfaces on a rotating horizontal diamond wheel kept wet by a constant flow of water that carries away silica dust. Diamond lathes are used to further cut and shape the glass as required.

Such "cold cut pieces" often have dull or matte finishes. Brightness and lustre is restored by further hand polishing with pumice and a putty of cerium oxide on wheels like the ones shown here. Steuben is the only contemporary glassmaker that does not use the shortcut of acid baths in the finishing process to restore surface shine.

A glassworker carefully compares the dimensions of a finished piece to its full-scale working drawing (left). In the exacting and time-consuming process of forming and finishing, each individual piece of Steuben crystal is touched by many pairs of human hands.

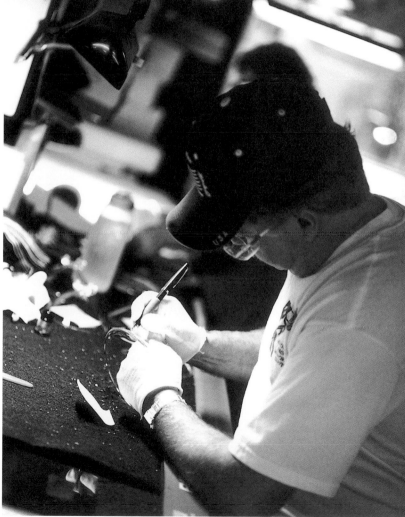

OPPOSITE The precise height of Taf Lebel Schaefer's finished Loyal Companion sculpture is carefully measured. Other inspectors (above) hold a Steuben bowl to the light to check for scratches, chips, or imperfections in the glass. If any are found, the piece is immediately destroyed.

RIGHT Only after a piece of crystal has been arduously inspected and deemed absolutely perfect is it signed "Steuben" with a diamond-lipped pen.

portfolio 4

Elephant, Handkerchief Vase, Little Handkerchief Vase, Petal-Cut Decanter, Tulip Champagne,
Tulip White Wine Glass, Deep Flower Bowl, Dolphin Hand Cooler, Rose Vase, Lyre Vase.

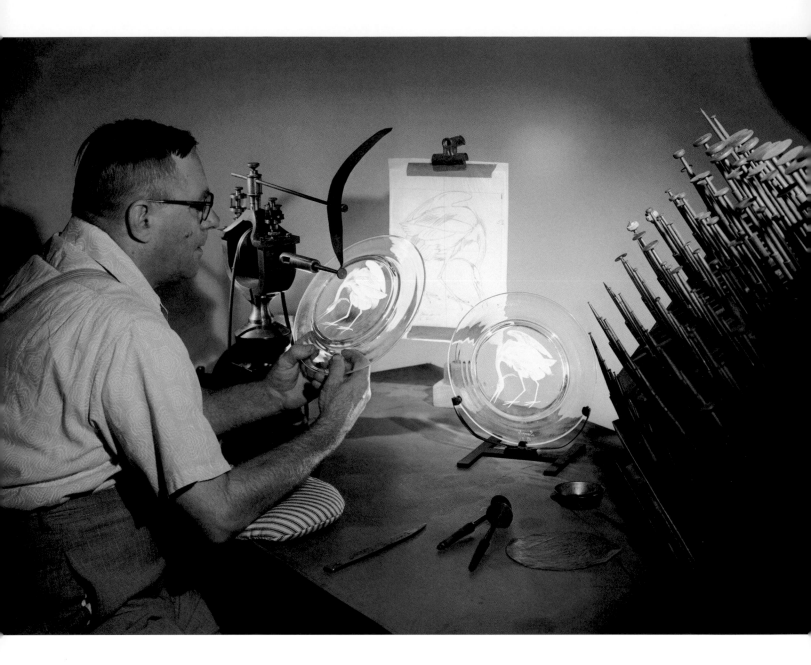

In a vintage photograph from the late 1940s, master craftsman
Ed Palme engraves a Great Blue Heron for the Audubon Plate series.
Guided by a shop drawing and finished plate, he interchanges many
handmade copper wheels of varying sizes on the rotating lathe to
achieve cuts of varying depth and thickness.

preserving the craft tradition

Steuben is renowned for its detailed copper-wheel engraving, an art first developed in the stone- and gem-cutting regions of 17th-century Bohemia. Adapted from rock crystal to glass, the wheel-engraving technique was handed down through generations of Bohemian craftsmen. In the late 19th century, many of these skilled European engravers emigrated to Corning, drawn by its growing glass-cutting industry, and set up shop in their own homes. During Steuben's first decades, Frederick Carder relied on these outside engravers, whose concentrated presence in Corning no doubt eased Steuben's 1933 transition from colored glass to colorless engraved crystal. By 1938, a dozen independent Corning engravers had been recruited to work directly for Steuben in its factory. Last to arrive was the virtuoso engraver Joseph Libisch, who worked on Steuben's most important pieces in the years that followed.

The process of copper-wheel engraving has changed little over time. With India ink, the artisan first sketches out the design on a polished glass blank, which is cut by pressing the glass against a rotating copper wheel affixed to a lathe. (An engraver may use as many as fifty interchangeable copper wheels of varying sizes, which he makes himself.) Viewed through the glass, the reverse side of these shallow or "intaglio" cuts creates the effect of a remarkably detailed three-dimensional sculpture. Each touch of glass to wheel must be accomplished with great delicacy and precision, because there is no way to cover up mistakes. In all of glassmaking history, there is no more time-intensive technique than copper-wheel engraving. A single piece often takes hundreds of hours to complete.

Steuben stands commited to preserving this increasingly rare, centuries-old art. It takes an apprentice at least six years to become adept enough to qualify as a full-fledged Steuben copper-wheel engraver. In 1985, to help extend the working years of its aging master engravers, Steuben outfitted their homes with fully equipped "north light" engraving studios. Today, as in the early 1900s, all of Steuben's engravers work primarily from home, but spend six weeks a year at the factory on a rotating basis so that visitors may continue to observe the fascinating process firsthand.

A detail of Sidney Waugh's hands as he sketches one element of his complex design for the Merry-Go-Round Bowl in correct position on the glass, ca. 1947.

OPPOSITE Guided by Waugh's shop drawing and with palpable concentration, the master engraver Joe Libisch, who came to work for Steuben in 1938, makes shallow intaglio cuts in the Merry-Go-Round Bowl.

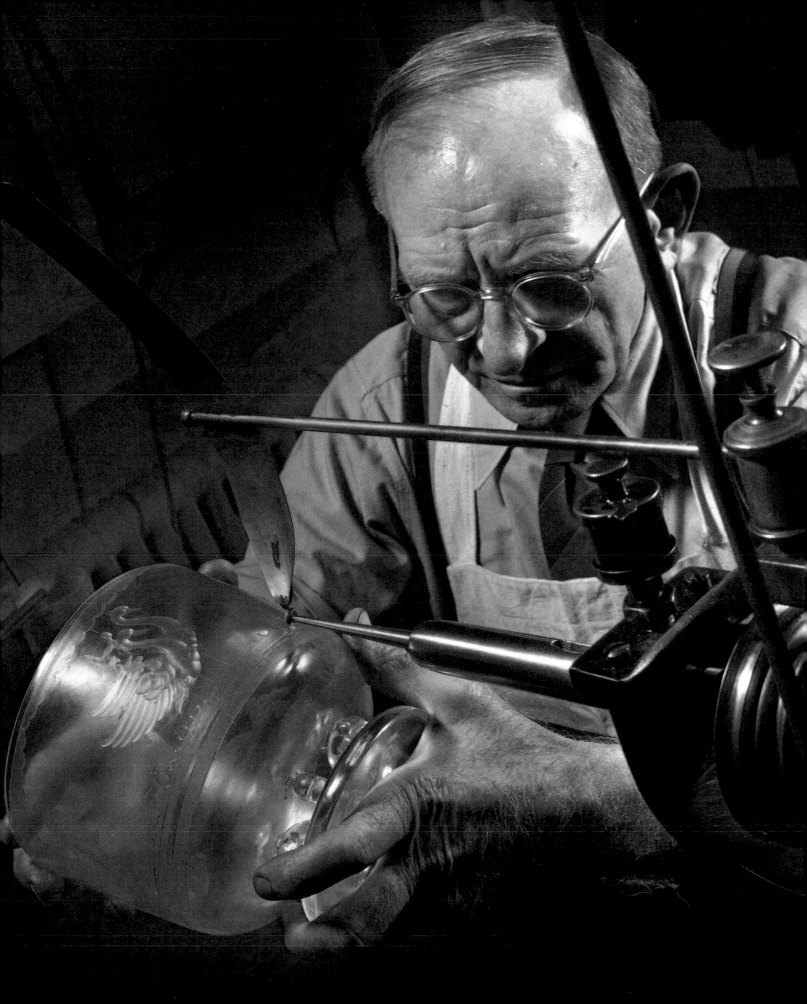

In this vintage photo, Libisch's hands are rock solid as he touches the Merry-Go-Round Bowl gently to the rotating wheel. In addition to exceptional artistic talent, great copper-wheel engravers like Libisch needed excellent coordination and enormous endurance to lift and accurately position the heavy crystal against the rotating wheel, often for hours at a time.

OPPOSITE Detailed with carousel figures of great depth and sculptural quality, the finished Merry-Go-Round Bowl is a consummate example of copper-wheel artistry. It was Steuben's first gift of state, presented by President Truman to Princess Elizabeth on the occasion of her marriage to Prince Philip in 1947.

Roger Selander, a third-generation Corning glassworker, is one of the artisans helping to preserve the art of copper-wheel engraving at Steuben as it embarks on its second century. Here he adds the final touches to an example of Sidney Waugh's Gazelle Bowl. It is still one of the company's most enduringly popular pieces.

OPPOSITE Steuben's best-known piece and its first example of copper-wheel engraving, Sidney Waugh's incomparable 1935 Gazelle Bowl is again in limited production.

portfolio 5

Low Teardrop Candlestick, Hellenic Urn, Olive Dish, Teardrop Deca Baluster Wine Glass.

President Dwight D. Eisenhower, with wife Mamie at his side, receives Steuben's Eisenhower Cup, presented by his cabinet to mark his first anniversary in office on January 20, 1954. The bowl is copper-wheel engraved with images commemorating highlights of the president's life and career. Cabinet members John Foster Dulles and Oveta Culp Hobby look on.

in good company

In the forty years following his 1933 reorganization of Steuben to focus on clear crystal, the patrician Arthur Houghton—an instinctive and tenacious marketer—worked constantly to publicize his modern new glass in the right circles. Steuben's tasteful advertisements appeared in the most fashionable magazines, while elegant cocktail parties, exhibitions, and charity benefits held at the Fifth Avenue shop gave Steuben an aura of sophistication and glamour that attracted socialites and celebrities alike.

Houghton tirelessly promoted Steuben's brilliant, American-made crystal to the White House and State Department for use as an official gift of state. His efforts met with great success. President Harry S. Truman gave Steuben's Merry-Go-Round Bowl to England's Princess Elizabeth on the occasion of her marriage to Prince Philip in 1947, and every occupant of the White House since then has selected Steuben crystal as an official gift of state. Today, Steuben is well established as the gift of choice not just for heads of state and political leaders, but also for top corporations and businesses as well as nonprofit organizations and eminent individuals in sports, medicine, and the performing arts. In 1989, Steuben was singularly honored to design and produce the prestigious Malcolm Baldrige Quality Award for corporate excellence, which is presented annually by the president of the United States.

President Lyndon B. Johnson and Paul Martin, Canada's minister for external affairs, peruse the Great Ring of Canada at Montreal's Expo '67. The best-known Steuben gift of state, this massive piece of crystal was commissioned by Johnson as a gift to Canadian prime minister Lester Pearson from the American people on the centenary of Canada's nationhood.

OPPOSITE Displayed throughout Canada's centennial year at the Montreal World's Fair, the forty-inch-high Great Ring of Canada, designed by Donald Pollard and Alexander Seidel and engraved by Steuben's master craftsmen Roland Ehrlacher and Ladislav Havlik, is composed of 12 engraved plaques and faceted spheres symbolizing Canada's ten provinces and two territories, arranged in a setting of rhodium-plated steel.

ABOVE LEFT Dr. Martin Luther King Jr. receives an engraved Steuben bowl, presented with appreciation by the citizens of Atlanta, Georgia, on January 27, 1965.

ABOVE RIGHT On her 1976 visit to Manhattan's historic Trinity Church, Queen Elizabeth II accepts a Steuben Covered Centerpiece containing 279 peppercorns in payment of the church's royal rent of one peppercorn annually, set by King William in 1697.

OPPOSITE Originally named The Hull and created in 1975 for a client who did not complete the purchase, the one-of-a-kind, elliptical Crusader's Bowl was designed by Zevi Blum and engraved in rare "hochschnitt," or high relief, by Steuben's Roland Ehrlacher. Priced at $75,000, it took 675 hours to engrave. In 1981, Nancy Reagan purchased it as the president's official wedding gift to Prince Charles and Lady Diana Spencer.

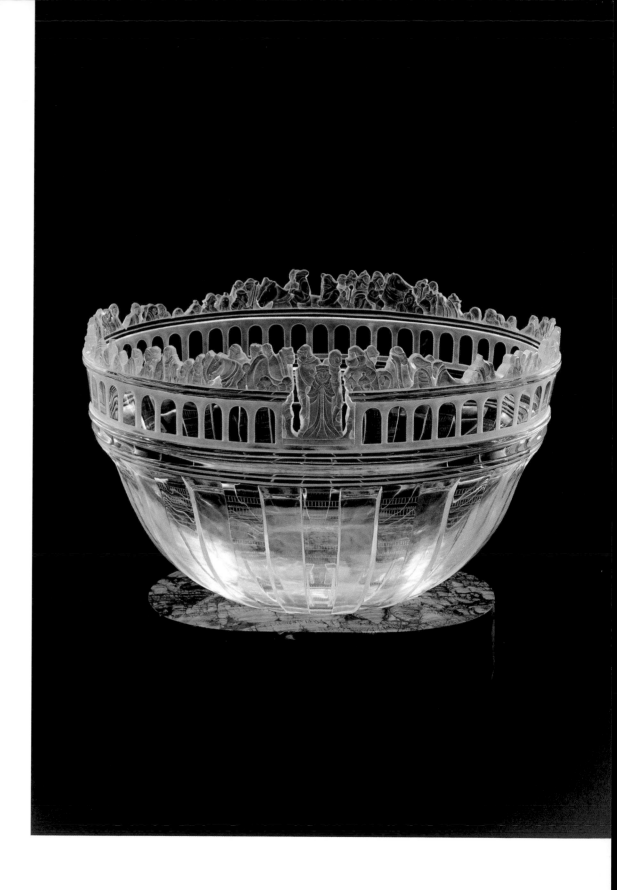

portfolio 6

Eagle, Young Heron, Graceful Heron, Owl Hand Cooler, Apple, Teardrop Candlesticks, Gander, Preening Goose.

masterworks

Alone among materials, glass has the ability to capture, reflect, and refract light. The remarkable optical qualities of pure crystal invite artistic experimentation. That is why, in addition to making functional and decorative designs for the table and home, Steuben has always supported the exploration of glass as a purely artistic medium.

Over the years, this commitment has fostered a series of major artworks by Steuben's own designers, as well as guest artists internationally renowned for their work in other media. Freed from marketing considerations and the constraints of product design, each of these masterworks is a testament to the unique qualities of Steuben crystal as well as the individuality and creativity of the artists who work with it.

Steuben's alliance with the fine arts began in 1927, when Henri Matisse offered to create a drawing to be engraved on a piece of Steuben. Other internationally renowned painters, sculptors, and printmakers were soon invited to do the same. Their commissioned sketches were engraved on Steuben vases, bowls, and plates for the landmark exhibition "Twenty-seven Artists in Crystal," which opened at the Fifth Avenue shop in 1940 with a star-studded list of participants including Georgia O'Keeffe, Aristide Maillol, Salvador Dalí, and Fernand Léger. In the 1950s, Steuben organized other high-caliber invitational exhibitions including "British Artists in Crystal" and "Asian Artists in Crystal," which traveled to major museums around the world.

In the 1960s and 1970s, Arthur Houghton commissioned the Steuben Masterworks series of eight extraordinarily lavish pieces combining engraved crystal with precious metals and gems in the tradition of Cellini and Fabergé. Designed by Steuben's senior staff artists in consortium with master engravers, jewelers, and goldsmiths, each masterwork in this series of one-of-a-kind showpieces required two to four years to complete.

By 1980, the aesthetic winds had shifted radically at Steuben. Top designers such as Eric Hilton, Peter Aldridge, and David Dowler experimented with new forming, precision cutting, and finishing techniques, abandoning narrative representations in favor of boldly abstract exhibition pieces that exalted the inherent qualities of the glass itself.

Of all the pieces in Steuben's 1940 "Twenty-seven Artists in Crystal" exhibition—conceived to celebrate the bonds between artist and artisan—Isamu Noguchi's simple cat, rendered in a few fluid strokes on the concave surface of a wide plate, was one of the most successful.

OPPOSITE The Unicorn and the Maiden, designed by Donald Pollard and engraved by Alexander Seidel as part of the Steuben Masterworks series, was embellished with 18-karat gold, ivory, diamonds, and sapphires. Inspired by the famous *Unicorn Tapestries* in the Cloisters of the Metropolitan Museum of Art, it was completed in 1971.

RIGHT Scenes from *A Midsummer Night's Dream* are framed in the Crown of Oberon, finished in 1981 after four years. Donald Pollard designed the glass, while illustrator Beni Montresor created drawings for master engraver Ladislav Havlik. Louis Feron fashioned the goldwork set with diamonds, emeralds, pearls, and a great tourmaline. It is the last of the Steuben Masterworks series.

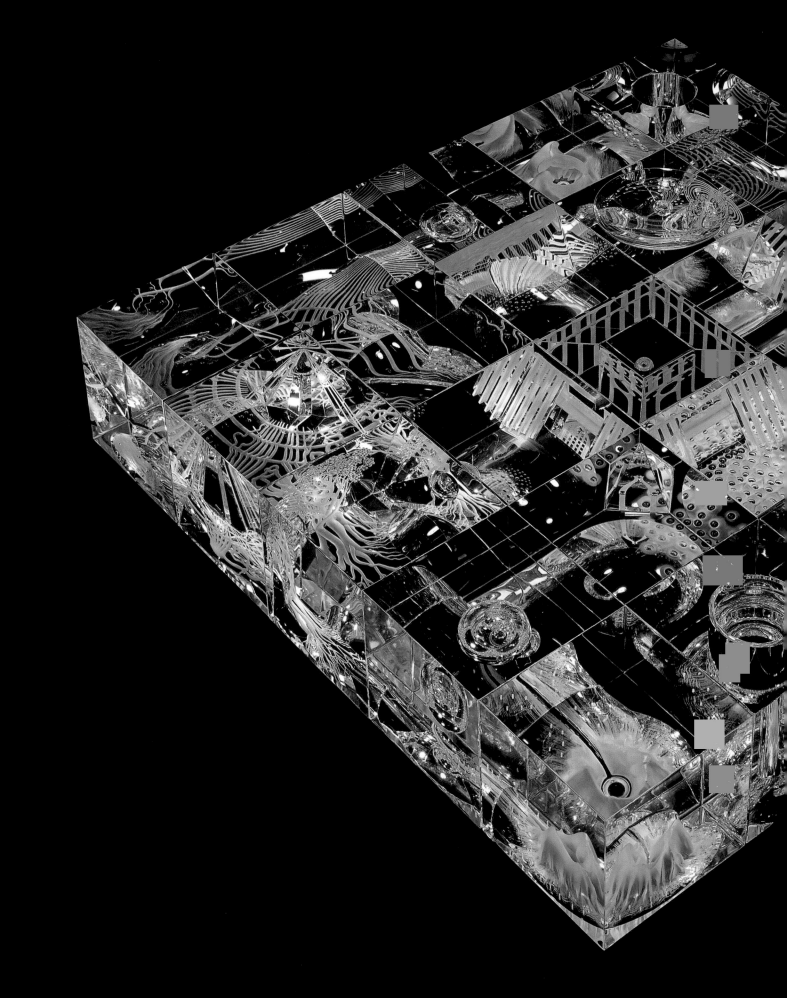

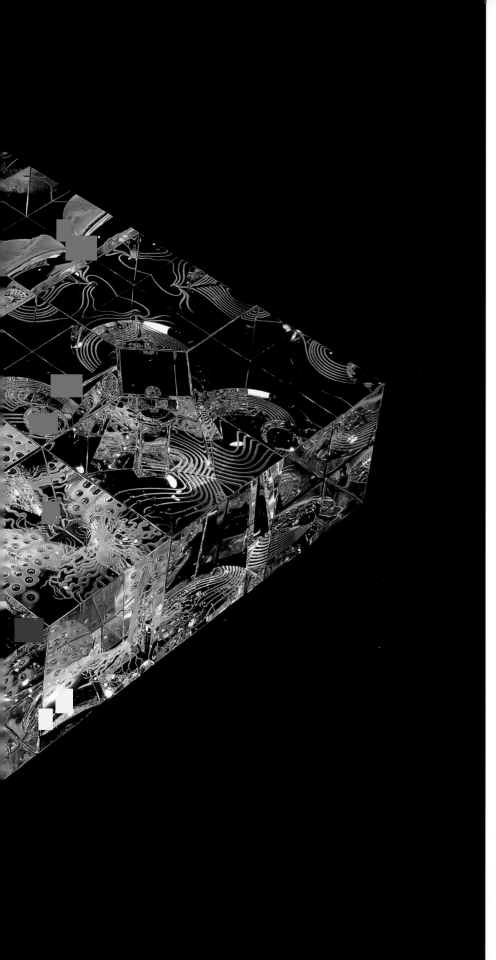

Completed in 1981, Eric Hilton's monumental Innerland, four years in the making, is a 17-inch-square modular landscape comprised of small engraved and sandblasted cubes expressing Hilton's concept of the unity of life and the inner being. It broke new ground for Steuben, both technically and aesthetically.

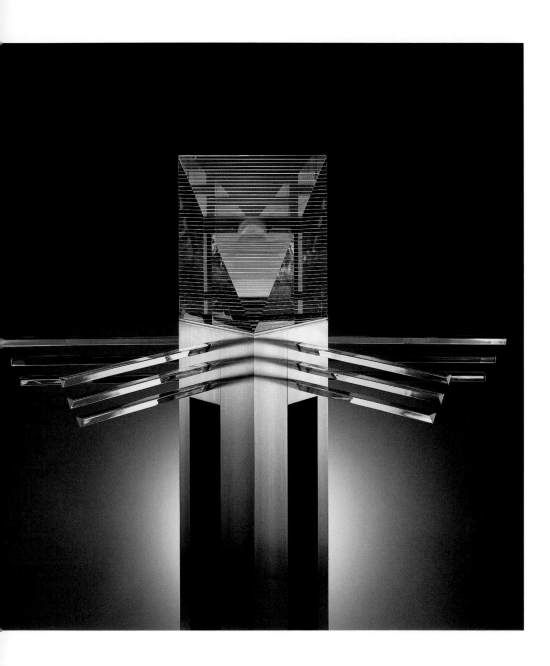

Designer Peter Aldridge created Sentinel for the "Steuben Project: Sculptures in Crystal" exhibition held at New York City's Heller Gallery in May 1988. Its precisely cut prismatic forms set into a metal base explore "the pure geometry of light" in a monumental 65-inch sculpture with commanding presence.

OPPOSITE Grotto—the daring centerpiece of David Dowler's technically stunning single-artist "Structure Revealed" exhibition of November 1997—incorporates two subtly colored lozenges of salmon-tinted and pale green glass, Steuben's first use of color since 1932. Like other Dowler pieces, the 22½-inch sculpture exploits the contrast of brilliantly polished and opaque, rough-cut crystal.

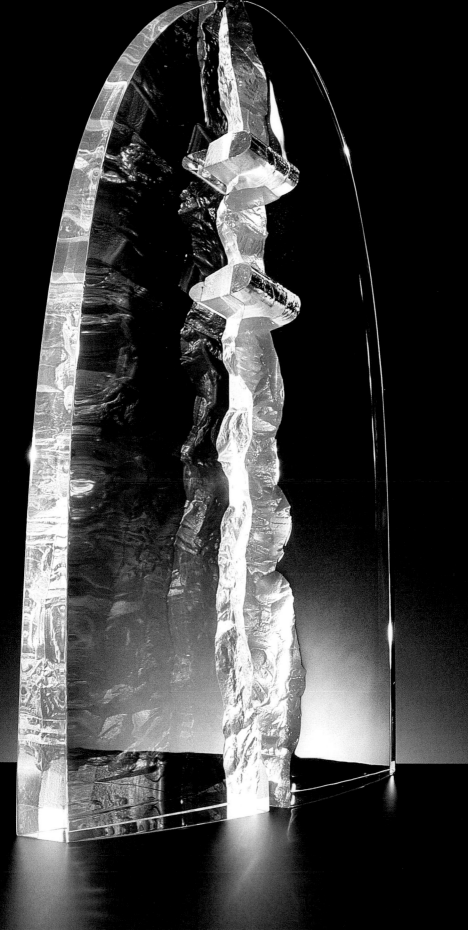

portfolio 7

Flower Vase, Low-Footed Bowl, Counterpoint Champagne Glass, Counterpoint Red Wine Glass, Horse Head Heavy-Cut Old-Fashioned Glass, Heavy-Cut Double Old-Fashioned Glass, Heavy-Cut Decanter.

the art of giving

Don Wier's engraved sculpture the Performing Arts — a gift from the New York Philharmonic to the trustees of Lincoln Center in September 1962 — glimmers in the background as First Lady Jacqueline Bouvier Kennedy greets Philharmonic conductor Leonard Bernstein at a Lincoln Center benefit.

"Not what we give, but what we share/For the gift without the giver is bare," wrote the poet James Russell Lowell in 1848. Unsurpassed in its ability to convey a heartfelt sentiment or capture the essence of a special moment, pure Steuben crystal elevates giving to a sublime art. From the smallest token of thanks or remembrance to the grandest one-of-a-kind sculpture, there is an artful Steuben design that perfectly expresses the giver's intentions and memorably celebrates life's pleasures and milestones.

Distinguished for more than half a century as an American gift of state, Steuben has frequently been presented to presidents, ambassadors, and royalty, including Queen Elizabeth II of England, whose official visits to the United States have traditionally been

recognized with a presidential gift of Steuben. It has become the gift of choice, as well, for great cultural and social institutions seeking to recognize their supporters and benefactors. And it is a tradition among America's top corporations to present Steuben to their employees, executives, and directors to applaud accomplishment or express gratitude for years of dedicated service.

Yet it is the person-to-person gift of Steuben — presented as an expression of love, appreciation, thanks, or celebration — that speaks most directly from the heart. Whether it is a whimsical hand cooler, a symbolic animal sculpture, traditional holiday ornament, pristine bowl, or stunning copper-wheel engraved showpiece, a thoughtful gift of Steuben will be displayed and cherished for years, a happy reminder of the occasion — and the person who chose the gift.

Inspired by Arthurian legend, James Houston's 1963 Excalibur letter knife and paperweight, detailed in silver and gold, can be inscribed with a special sentiment on the sword's blade.

OPPOSITE For a dedicated angler or sportsman, renowned wildlife designer James Houston's Trout & Fly is an ideal gift. This 1963 classic is detailed with a Coachman fly of pure gold.

OPPOSITE Elegant in its
pristine simplicity, Angus
McDougall's iconic Apple—
symbol of New York City and
other splendid temptations—
has been one of Steuben's
most versatile gifts since its
introduction in 1940.

ABOVE Symbol of domestic
felicity, Lloyd Atkins's 1983
Cat Hand Cooler is a favorite
wedding gift.

RIGHT In Star Stream, a popular sculpture designed by Neil
Cohen in 1988, a shimmering
trail of light links two sparkling
stars to suggest the bond
between kindred spirits—or
partners in business.

Brought back into the line in
2002 as a Steuben Heritage
Reintroduction to mark James
Houston's 40th year with
Steuben, Mouse & Cheese—
detailed in pure 18-karat gold—
is prized by Houston collectors.

OPPOSITE James Houston's
classic 1975 Arctic Fisherman,
detailed in silver, is one of many
pieces inspired by this master
designer's 12-year sojourn in
the Arctic, where he lived and
worked with the Inuit people.

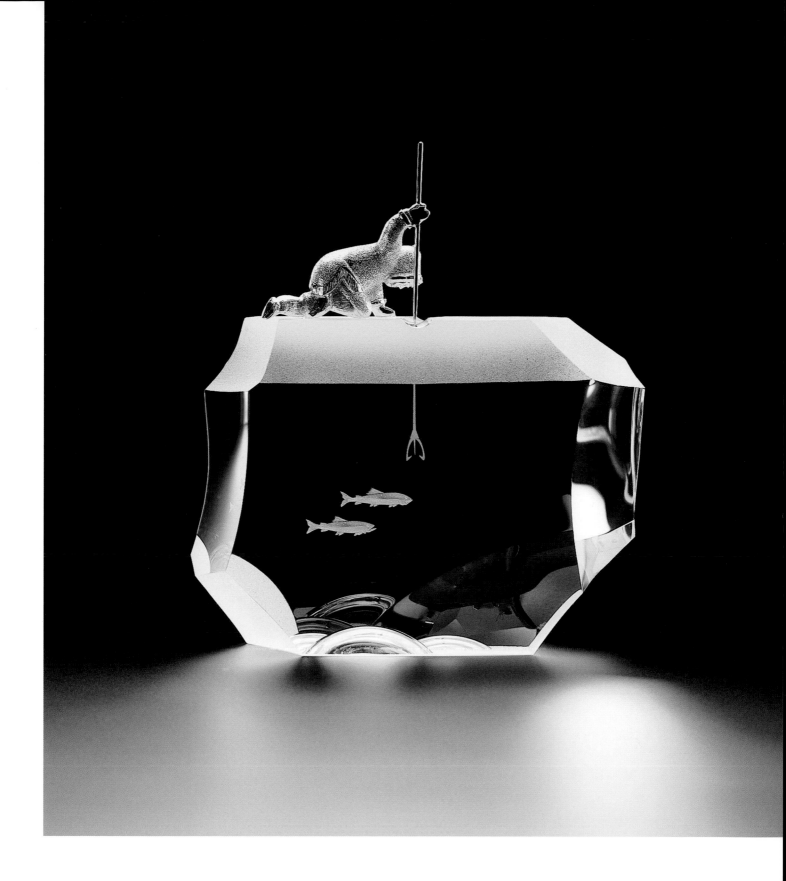

portfolio 8

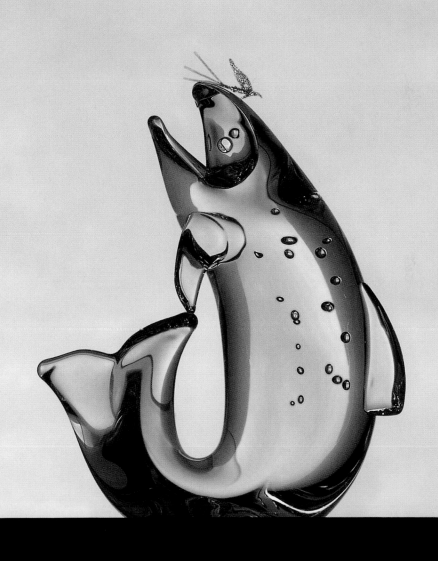

Trout & Fly, Lighthouse, Arctic Fisherm

collectible art

In the seven decades since 1933, when Steuben first introduced the color-free crystal that is its signature today, a growing legion of collectors and museums has come to prize this inimitably pure and brilliant hand-formed glass. Many collect Steuben because they appreciate the rare technical virtuosity inherent in its copper-wheel engraved exhibition pieces—each one the product of a meticulous, centuries-old, time-intensive craft now practiced and preserved in few places other than the Steuben factory in Corning, New York.

Some collectors seek out classic functional pieces of Steuben designed in the modernist aesthetic of the 1940s and 1950s. Still others take pleasure in building collections around a particular theme—animals, cityscapes, golf, or boating, for example—or they indulge a taste for the works of individual Steuben designers like George Thompson, Lloyd Atkins, and James Houston. Houston, a Steuben associate since 1962, has

an avid following of collectors who eagerly anticipate each minutely detailed new Arctic or wildlife design introduced by this prolific artist, adventurer, and storyteller.

To meet the growing demand for hard-to-find classics by these and other top designers, Steuben initiated the Heritage series in 1978. At regular intervals, a few carefully selected favorites from decades past are brought back into the line as Steuben Reintroductions. In addition to Steuben's diamond-pen signature, these pieces are inscribed with a second mark to distinguish them from original editions.

Over the years, examples of Steuben's glass artistry have been acquired not just by individual collectors, but by important museums in the Unites States and abroad—New York City's Metropolitan Museum of Art and Museum of Modern Art, the Art Institute of Chicago, the Cleveland Museum of Art, the Detroit Art Institute, and the Victoria and Albert Museum in London among them. Now, at the threshold of its second century, Steuben continues to foster its long-standing tradition of creating major sculptural works of museum caliber, and remains committed to preserving the centuries-old art of copper-wheel engraving for generations yet to come.

John Keenen of Keenen/ Riley designed the installation for the exhibition of historical Steuben, "Glass + Glamour: Steuben's Modern Moment, 1930–1960," on view at the Museum of the City of New York from November 2003 through April 2004.

Introduced in 2001, Eric Hilton's Dragonfly is a study in contrasts and a tribute to the engraver's skill. Within a hand-polished dome of solid crystal, the dragonfly's lacy wings are set off by the deft shading of its body and the bright spate of bubbles rising from the base.

OPPOSITE Designed by James Houston to commemorate his 40th year with Steuben in 2002, African Zebras is diamond-wheel cut in the shape of Kilimanjaro's snowy peaks. A zebra family is copper-wheel engraved in the foreground.

Designed by George Thompson
in 1955, Cathedral exploits the
refractive magic of Steuben crystal to create the illusion of an
ever-changing panoply of Gothic
architectural details and stately
apostles within a prismatic spire.

OPPOSITE Paul Schulze was
Steuben's director of design
in 1984 when he conceived the
iconic sculpture New York,
New York as the centerpiece of
Steuben's landmark exhibition
"50 Years on Fifth."

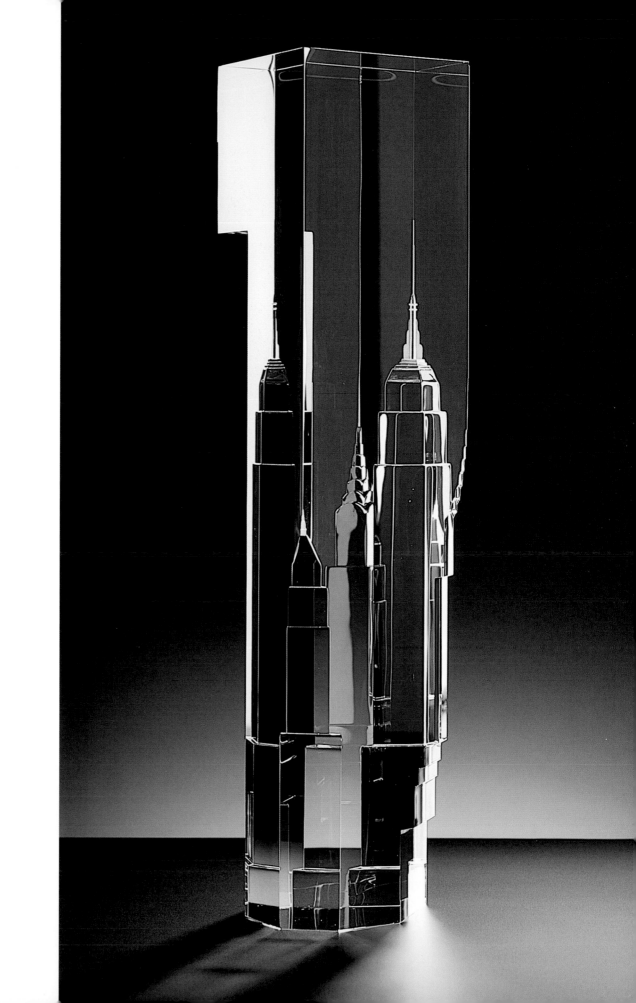

OPPOSITE Inspired by the Herman Melville classic, Donald Pollard and Sidney Waugh's dramatic sculpture Moby Dick marked a design milestone for Steuben in 1959. It is the first piece in which the copper-wheel engraving is not just an applied decoration, but is integral to the form itself.

RIGHT Designed by Peter Aldridge and Jane Osborn-Smith in 1985, Swan Bowl is prized as a virtuoso example of Steuben's techniques of blowing, cutting, polishing, and copper-wheel engraving. It is limited to an edition of 50.

135

portfolio captions

PORTFOLIO 1

Glimmer Old-Fashioned Glass, Joel Smith, 2003; Glimmer Highball Glass, Joel Smith, 2003; Taffeta Vase, Joel Smith, 2003; Teardrop Bud Vase, David Hills, 1949; Small Folded Bowl, Joel Smith, 1993; Bouquet Vase, George Thompson, 1949; Small Orbit Bowl, Joel Smith, 2000; Classic Highball Glass, Joel Smith, 2003; Classic Old-Fashioned Glass, Joel Smith, 2003.

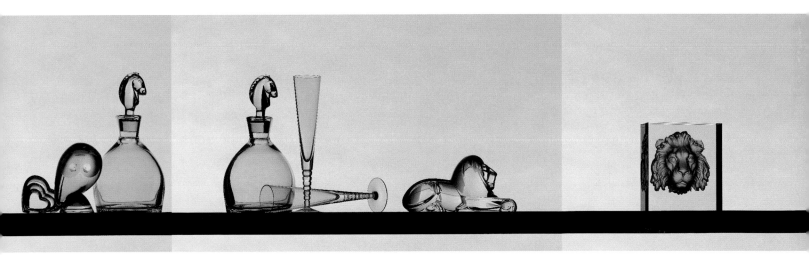

PORTFOLIO 2

Forever More, Eric Hilton, 2001; Owl, Donald Pollard, 1955; Equestrian Decanter, David Dowler, 2003; Evening Champagne, Dante Marioni, 2003; Lion, Lloyd Atkins, 1986; Regal Lion, Peter Drobny & Bill Sullivan, 1996.

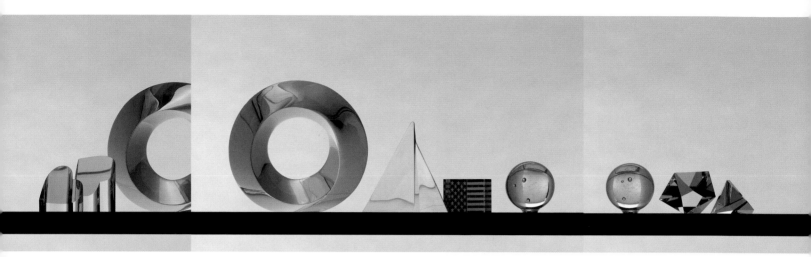

PORTFOLIO 3

Heart Point Down, James Carpenter, 1979; Heart Point Up, James Carpenter, 1979; Mobius Prism, Peter Drobny, 1993; Sailboat, Peter Aldridge, 1989; Stars and Stripes, Peter Aldridge, 2001; Galaxy, Donald Pollard, 1980; Rising Star, Robert Cassetti, 1991; Trigon, Peter Aldridge, 1985.

PORTFOLIO 4

Elephant, James Houston, 1964; Handkerchief Vase, Steuben Design Team, 1991; Little Handkerchief Vase, Steuben Design Team, 1991; Petal-Cut Decanter, Gerald Gulotta, 2003; Tulip Champagne Glass, Gerald Gulotta, 2003; Tulip White Wine Glass, Gerald Gulotta, 2003; Deep Flower Bowl, Donald Pollard, 1959; Dolphin Hand Cooler, Lloyd Atkins, 1996; Rose Vase, George Thompson, 1959; Lyre Vase, Lloyd Atkins, 1962.

PORTFOLIO 5

Low Teardrop Candlestick, David Hills, 1949; Hellenic Urn, Robert Cassetti, 1990; Olive Dish, John Dreves, 1939; Teardrop Decanter, Joel Smith, 2003; Baluster Water Goblet, George Thompson, 1940; Baluster Wine Glass, George Thompson, 1940.

PORTFOLIO 6

Eagle, James Houston, 1964; Young Heron, Taf Lebel Schaefer, 2000; Graceful Heron, Taf Lebel Schaefer, 2000; Owl Hand Cooler, Lloyd Atkins, 1981; Apple, Angus McDougall, 1940; Teardrop Candlesticks, F.B. Sellew, 1937; Gander, Lloyd Atkins, 1976; Preening Goose, Lloyd Atkins, 1977.

PORTFOLIO 7

Flower Vase, George Thompson, 1942; Low-Footed Bowl, John Dreves, 1942; Counterpoint Champagne Glass, Dante Marioni, 2002; Counterpoint Red Wine Glass, Dante Marioni, 2002; Horse Head, Sidney Waugh, 1937; Heavy-Cut Old-Fashioned Glass, Joel Smith, 2003; Heavy-Cut Double Old-Fashioned Glass, Joel Smith, 2003; Heavy-Cut Decanter, Joel Smith, 2003.

PORTFOLIO 8

Trout & Fly, James Houston, 1966; Lighthouse, David Dowler, 1993; Arctic Fisherman, James Houston, 1973; Excalibur, James Houston, 1963; Moby Dick, Donald Pollard & Sidney Waugh, 1959.

collecting vintage steuben

There are two major categories of vintage Steuben glass: the many types of colored, cased, cut, and acid-etched glass designed by Frederick Carder in the years between 1903 and 1933 (popularly known as "Carder Glass"); and the flawlessly pure, colorless crystal made at Steuben in the years following 1933, when Arthur Amory Houghton Jr. took Carder's place at the company's helm. The extraordinary clarity and brilliance of post-1933 Steuben crystal—along with the peerless craftsmanship inherent in its forming and decoration—are instantly recognized hallmarks that make it a sought-after collectible. Each piece of glass that leaves the factory is guaranteed to be flawless, and is signed "Steuben" with a diamond-tipped pen. Pieces that do not measure up to Steuben's standard of uncompromising excellence are destroyed, ensuring the enduring value of each perfect, signed object.

On average, about 30 new Steuben designs have been introduced in each year since 1933, and a few have remained in production for many decades. Others have been retired after a few years to make way for new designs in Steuben's ongoing aesthetic evolution. In 1978 the company initiated the practice of bringing a select few classic favorites back into the line from time to time as part of the Heritage series. Many of Steuben's complex copper-wheel engraved designs have been issued in strictly limited and numbered editions; the rarity of such small-edition pieces increases their value to collectors over time. Pieces accompanied by their original Steuben packaging—the signature grey flannel bags and linen boxes, or for major engraved designs, the elegant fitted red leather cases—are especially desirable.

Collectors seek out pieces of vintage Steuben—as well as historic Steuben publications, catalogues, and other ephemera—at fine antique shows and estate sales, and through internet auctions such as the ones conducted by eBay. Vintage Steuben may also be acquired from, sold through, and appraised by antiques dealers who specialize in glass or twentieth-century decorative arts. A list of such dealers is available on request from Steuben's customer service department (1-800-STEUBEN). From time to time, vintage pieces of Steuben will also be made available for purchase at Steuben's flagship store at 667 Madison Avenue in New York City. Call to inquire.

For collectors of pre-1933 Steuben the definitive reference is *Frederick Carder and Steuben Glass: American Classics* by Thomas P. Dimitroff (Schiffer Publishing Ltd., 1998). The comprehensive guide for collectors of colorless post-1933 Steuben crystal is Mary Jean Madigan's *Steuben Glass: An American Tradition in Crystal*, first published by Harry N. Abrams in 1982 and now available in an enlarged, revised, and updated edition released by Abrams in 2003.

OPPOSITE Lloyd Atkins conceived this classic Steuben Cruet (left) in 1954, while the Twist-stem Gold Aurene Candlestick at right accompanied a set of tableware designed by Frederick Carder in the 1920s.

acknowledgments

This book, like so many good things involving Steuben Glass in its centenary year, reflects the contributions of many talented individuals whose passion for excellence reflects Steuben's own. Foremost among them are Steuben's president and CEO Marie McKee and director of design and marketing Robert Cassetti, whose shared vision has illuminated this project from its inception. General manager Peter J. Aagaard advised on the selection of glassmaking images from among many striking documentary shots captured onsite by photographer Stewart Ferebee, while operations manager Connie J. Lapp read the production captions for accuracy. Administrative coordinators Shelley Pierri and Nedra Jumper patiently arranged schedules and visits to the plant. Steuben product design manager Joel Smith and director of visual presentation Mark Tamayo organized the glass for photographer Jay Zukerkorn's remarkable portfolio of images. In Corning, access to rare photographs was generously provided by Michelle Cotton, director of the Corning Incorporated Division of Archives and Records Maintenance; while at the Rakow Library of the Corning Museum of Glass, reference librarian Gail Bardhan rounded up many key images and documents. Photo research was spearheaded by CIDARM associate Kris Gable, whose tenacity, perception, and (quite literally) photographic memory brought to light many wonderful images. Steuben's Jennifer Privette and Patricia Marti kindly advised on still other needs. At Pentagram, Abbott Miller's peerless design direction was expertly supported by the efforts of Johnschen Kudos and Jess Mackta. At Harry N. Abrams, senior editor Andrea Danese ably synchronized the entire effort along with production manager Maria Pia Gramaglia, while editor-in-chief Eric Himmel provided wisdom and support. To each of these talented and generous individuals—and to my family—I am deeply grateful.

M.J. Madigan

photo credits

Associated Press page 88. **Brown Brothers** pages 36, 37. **A. Bruno & Associates** page 40. **Michael Caputo** page 39 (right). **Corning Glass Works** pages 28, 31, 32, 33. **Courtesy Corning Incorporated** pages 30, 39 (left), 41, 42, 45, 46, 74, 76–80, 91, 102, 107, 114, 134, 143. **Courtesy The Corning Museum of Glass** page 100. **Frank Ehrenford** page 35. **Joyce Fay** page 2. **Stewart Ferebee** pages 54, 56–67. **Gaffer News** page 92 (left). **Gottscho-Schleisner** page 44. **Jim Hale** page 92 (right). **Elliott Kaufman** page 47. **Robert Moore** pages 16–21, 81, 93, 103, 104–105, 106, 116–121, 130–133, 135. **John Rawlings/Vogue © Condé Nast Publications Inc.** page 14. **Annie Schlechter** page 128. **Ezra Stoller © Esto** page 43. **Underwood & Underwood** pages 34, 38. **United Press International Photo** page 90. **Jay Zukerkorn** jacket and pages 9–12, 23–26, 49–52, 69–72, 83–86, 95–98, 109–112, 123–126, 137–140.